Children's First
Space
ENCYCLOPEDIA

Written by
Claudia Martin

Consultant: Dr. Helen Giles

ARCTURUS

ARCTURUS

This edition published in 2022 by Arcturus Publishing Limited
26/27 Bickels Yard, 151–153 Bermondsey Street,
London SE1 3HA

Copyright © Arcturus Holdings Limited

Author: Claudia Martin
Designer: Lorraine Inglis
Consultant: Dr. Helen Giles
Editor: Becca Clunes
Design manager: Jessica Holliland
Managing editor: Joe Harris

ISBN: 978-1-3988-1995-5
CH010045NT
Supplier 29, Date 0522, Print run 00000998

Printed in China

Children's First
Space
ENCYCLOPEDIA

CONTENTS

SUPER SPACE

We live on a small, rocky planet named Earth. Our planet is just one of 100 billion planets in our galaxy, and there are 100 billion galaxies in the Universe. The Universe is really huge! In fact, as far as we know, the Universe is everything that exists.

Sparkling Stars

From Earth, you can see about 500 stars at night, but astronomers know that there are many, many more. Stars are glowing balls of gas, which we can see in the night sky as twinkling lights.

Our nearest star, the Sun, is 15 million °C (27 million °F) at its core.

Astronaut Stephen Robinson spacewalks 400 km (250 miles) above Earth.

Pulling Planets

A planet is a large object that is spinning around a star. A planet's gravity has pulled it into a ball. Gravity is a force that pulls all objects toward each other. Big objects pull much harder than small objects.

A chunk of space rock needs to be at least 600 km (370 miles) wide before it pulls itself into a ball.

Huge Universe

The Universe is so large that astronomers need to use large measurements to keep track of it. Distances are often measured in light years. One light year is how far light can travel in a year: 9.46 trillion km (5.88 trillion miles).

When you look at a star, its light may have taken thousands of years to reach your eyes.

THE SOLAR SYSTEM

In the middle of our Solar System is a star named the Sun. This ball of hot gas gives us light and heat. The Solar System is all the planets, moons, rocks, and ice that spin around the Sun.

JUPITER

ASTEROID BELT

SUN

MERCURY

VENUS

EARTH

MARS

The planets travel around the Sun on a curved path, named an orbit.

THE SOLAR SYSTEM
SIZE: 27 billion km
(16.8 billion miles) across
DISTANCE FROM MIDDLE OF MILKY
WAY GALAXY: 27,000 light years
KNOWN PLANETS: 8

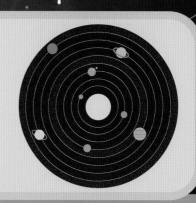

Birth of the Planets

Around 4.5 billion years ago, a cloud of gas and dust was spinning around the young Sun. Clumps formed in the cloud. As the clumps grew, their gravity pulled in more material—making planets.

It took millions of years for the planets to form.

SATURN

URANUS

NEPTUNE

The planets are held in orbit by the Sun's gravity.

Heavy or Light

The four inner planets are made of heavier materials than the outer planets. Lighter materials were blown away from the Sun into the outer Solar System, where Jupiter, Saturn, Uranus, and Neptune formed.

KEY:
1. Solid metal inner core
2. Liquid metal outer core
3. Partly melted rock
4. Solid rock

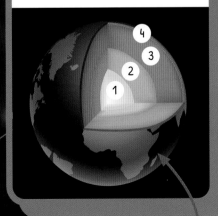

Earth and the other inner planets are made of metal and rock.

KEY:
1. Rocky core
2. Metallic hydrogen
3. Liquid hydrogen
4. Hydrogen gas

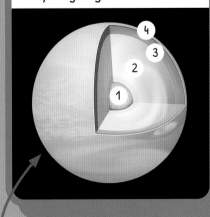

Jupiter and the other outer planets contain icy or gassy materials, such as hydrogen.

MERCURY

Mercury is the smallest of the Solar System's eight planets. It orbits closest to the Sun, giving it the shortest and fastest orbit. It takes only 88 days to travel around the Sun, at a speed of 47 km (27 miles) per second.

These streaks are dust thrown out by a space rock crash.

Crashing Craters

Mercury's surface is covered in craters. These were made billions of years ago when space rocks called comets and asteroids crashed into the planet.

This photo shows the different heights of Mercury's surface in different shades, with purple for the lowest areas and red for the highest.

Crinkling Wrinkles

Today, Mercury's surface is around 167 °C (332 °F), much warmer than Earth's average 15 °C (59 °F). Like the other inner planets, Mercury was hotter when it first formed, due to its rocks smashing together really hard! As the planet's core has cooled, it has shrunk a little, making Mercury's surface wrinkle.

In this photo, we can see Mercury's wrinkles running between and through its craters.

This crater, named the Caloris Basin, is 1,550 km (963 miles) wide.

MERCURY
SIZE: 4,880 km (3,032 miles) across
DISTANCE FROM THE SUN:
   57.9 million km (36 million miles)
KNOWN MOONS: 0

Mercury   Earth

VENUS

Like all the planets, Venus turns around its own axis (a line through its middle) as it orbits the Sun. Venus has the slowest rotation of all the planets: One turn takes 243 days.

VENUS
SIZE: 12,104 km (7,521 miles) across
DISTANCE FROM THE SUN:
    108.2 million km (67.2 million miles)
KNOWN MOONS: 0

Venus   Earth

Dark areas are old, cooled lava flows.

Bad Atmosphere

Like Earth, Venus is surrounded by a blanket of gases, called an atmosphere. Most of Venus's atmosphere is carbon dioxide gas, which traps the Sun's heat. This makes Venus the hottest Solar System planet, with an average surface temperature of 460 °C (860 °F).

On Earth, our clouds are made of water droplets, but on Venus clouds are made of sulfuric acid droplets. Lightning flickers from the clouds to the baking ground.

These bright, pale areas are mountains.

Towering Volcanoes

Venus has more volcanoes than any other planet: more than 1,600. Astronomers have never seen one of these volcanoes erupt, but space probes have spotted signs of eruptions, such as flows of melted rock called lava.

Venus's highest volcano is Maat Mons, which is 8 km (5 miles) tall.

11

EARTH

Earth is a special planet because it is the perfect distance from its star! At this distance, Earth is warm enough for its water to flow— rather than all freeze into ice or sizzle into steam. Without Earth's oceans, rivers, and rain, there would be no animals and plants!

This photo of Earth was taken from onboard *Apollo 8*.

Days and Years

Earth turns around its axis, making one rotation every 24 hours. When one side of Earth is facing the Sun, it has daylight. When that side faces away from the Sun, it has night. As well as rotating on its axis, Earth also travels around the Sun. It takes 365.25 days to make one orbit. Earth's axis is slightly tilted. When the northern half, or hemisphere, of Earth is tilted toward the Sun, it has summer. When the northern hemisphere is tilted away from the Sun, it has winter.

Summer brings warmer weather and longer days.

EARTH

AXIS

SUN

Summer in the southern hemisphere

Summer in the northern hemisphere

In 1968, *Apollo 8* was the first spacecraft to orbit the Moon.

EARTH

SIZE: 12,742 km (7,918 miles) across
DISTANCE FROM THE SUN: 149.6 million km
(93 million miles)
KNOWN MOONS: 1

Earth 🌍   Sun

Airy Atmosphere

Earth's gravity holds a mixture of gases, called air, around it. Air contains oxygen, which animals need to breathe. Scientists divide Earth's atmosphere into layers, each less tightly packed with air than the one below.

Many satellites orbit in the exosphere.

Particles from the Sun make lights known as auroras.

Small space rocks burn up here, making "shooting stars."

Planes soar among the clouds of the troposphere.

Weather balloons float here to measure conditions.

KEY:

1. Exosphere:
   10,000 km
   (6,200 miles)

2. Thermosphere:
   500 km (300 miles)

3. Mesosphere:
   80 km (50 miles)

4. Stratosphere:
   40 km (25 miles)

5. Troposphere:
   10 km (6 miles)

THE MOON

The Moon has been orbiting our planet since Earth was around 100 million years old. The dark areas we can see on the Moon, sometimes called "seas," are hardened lava that was spewed from long-ago volcanoes.

THE MOON
SIZE: 3,476 km (2,160 miles) across
DISTANCE FROM EARTH: 384,402 km (238,856 miles)
ORBIT AROUND EARTH: 27 days

Moon　　　Earth

This crater, named Tycho, was made 108 million years ago.

The Sea of Serenity is 674 km (419 miles) wide.

Making the Moon

Most astronomers think the Moon was made when another planet crashed into the young Earth. The crash sent rock and metal shooting into space. Earth's gravity held this material in orbit, where it collected into the Moon.

Astronomers have named the planet that crashed into Earth: Theia.

THEIA

CRASH

YOUNG EARTH

ORBITING MATERIAL

ORBITING MOON

Full Moon to New Moon

As the Moon orbits Earth once a month, it appears to change shape. This is because we can see only the side of the Moon that is lit by the Sun, while the rest is in shadow.

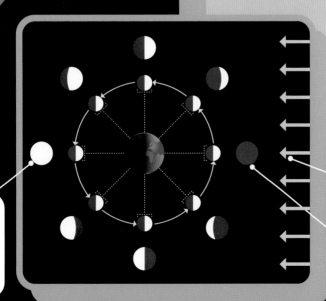

SUNLIGHT

When we see all the Moon's lit side, we see a "Full Moon."

When we see almost none of the Moon's lit side, we see a "New Moon."

15

MARS

Today, Mars is a dry and lifeless planet. But astronomers think the planet once had oceans like Earth's. They even wonder if—long ago—Mars might have been home to tiny living things.

The cold north pole is covered by ice.

Signs of Life?

Astronomers can see that some of Mars's rocks were worn away by waves and rivers. On Earth, the oceans were where life began, around 4 billion years ago. If Mars's oceans were home to living things, no sign of them has been found—so far!

The *Perseverance* rover took this photo on Mars. Mars's rocks are red and dusty because they contain iron, which can rust—turning red—like old metal.

MARS

SIZE: 6,779 km (4,212 miles) across
DISTANCE FROM THE SUN:
  227.9 million km (141.6 million miles)
KNOWN MOONS: 2

Mars   Earth

On the equator, Mars never gets hotter than 20 °C (68 °F).

Phobos and Deimos

Mars has two small moons: Phobos, just 22 km (14 miles) wide; and Deimos, which is 12 km (8 miles) wide. Astronomers think the moons might be space rocks, called asteroids, that were captured by the planet's gravity.

Phobos orbits closer to its planet than any other moon: just 6,000 km (3,700 miles) away. Deimos orbits 23,460 km (14,580 miles) from Mars.

17

THE ASTEROID BELT

Asteroids are made of rock and metal. Millions of them are circling the Sun between the orbits of Mars and Jupiter. Most asteroids are tiny, but more than 1 million are wider than 1 km (0.6 miles).

Asteroid Attack!

Most asteroids orbit in the Asteroid Belt, but around 27,000 have orbits that cross Earth's. Astronomers watch these asteroids closely. If a big asteroid comes to near, they will fly a space probe into it—knocking the asteroid off course!

Scientists think an asteroid 10 km (6 miles) wide hit Earth 66 million years ago, creating fires and dust clouds that wiped out the dinosaurs.

Asteroids are material left over from the formation of the planets.

The Asteroid Belt is 180 million km (112 million miles) wide.

Ceres the Dwarf Planet

The largest asteroid is named Ceres. Astronomers say Ceres is a dwarf planet. A dwarf planet is large enough for its gravity to pull it into a ball. Unlike a true planet, it is not large enough to clear other objects out of its orbit.

This photo of Ceres was taken by the *Dawn* space probe. We can see Ceres's bright crater, named Occator.

CERES
SIZE: 940 km (580 miles) across
DISTANCE FROM THE SUN:
   413.8 million km (257 million miles)
KNOWN MOONS: 0

Ceres   Earth

19

JUPITER

The Solar System's largest planet is mostly swirling hydrogen. In Jupiter's outer layers, the hydrogen is a gas but—deeper inside—it is pressed and heated into a flowing liquid. Like all the outer planets, Jupiter does not have a solid surface!

JUPITER

SIZE: 142,984 km (88,846 miles) across
DISTANCE FROM THE SUN:
    778.5 million km (483.7 million miles)
KNOWN MOONS: 79

Jupiter   Earth

Jupiter is rotating at 45,000 km (28,000 miles) per hour.

Super Storm!

Jupiter's super-fast rotation makes winds of up to 539 km (335 miles) per hour. These winds help to create huge storms. The largest, known as the Great Red Spot, is 16,000 km (9,900 miles) wide.

The Great Red Spot is red because Jupiter's clouds contain chemicals such as ammonia.

Jupiter's speedy spin creates bands of red cloud.

Biggest Moon

Jupiter's largest moon, Ganymede, is also the Solar System's largest. It is 5,268 km (3,273 miles) wide, bigger than the planet Mercury. Astronomers think a saltwater ocean may lie beneath Ganymede's icy surface.

Jupiter's four largest moons are the first, third, fourth, and sixth largest in the Solar System. Saturn's Titan comes second, while our Moon comes fifth.

GANYMEDE

CALLISTO

EUROPA

SATURN

Saturn is the most distant planet that we can see in the night sky without a telescope. Like the other planets, apart from Earth, it was named after a Greek or Roman god. Saturn was the Roman god of farming.

This gap between rings is named the Cassini Division.

Shining Rings

All four of the outer planets have rings, which are made of chunks of rock and ice. Saturn's rings are the largest and brightest, stretching up to 400,000 km (248,550 miles) from the planet's equator.

This photo has been tinted to show the size of the chunks in the rings. Purple areas contain chunks bigger than 5 cm (2 in) wide. Green areas contain smaller pieces.

Saturn is made mostly of hydrogen and helium.

SATURN
SIZE: 120,536 km (74,898 miles) across
DISTANCE FROM THE SUN:
1.4 billion km (890 million miles)
KNOWN MOONS: 82

Saturn   Earth

Many Moons

Saturn has 82 moons, more than any other planet. The largest is Titan, 5,149 km (3,200 miles) wide. Saturn also has many icy moonlets, smaller than 500 m (1,640 ft) across, which orbit among the rings.

This photo of Titan was taken by the *Cassini* space probe. The moon has a warm underground ocean that might be home to life!

URANUS

Uranus and Neptune are made mostly of three chemicals: water, ammonia, and methane. The methane makes Uranus look greenish blue. Although the planet's surface is cold, its rocky core reaches 5,000 °C (9,000 °F).

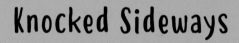

URANUS

SUN

Knocked Sideways

Unlike the other planets, Uranus orbits the Sun on its side, with its rings pointing upward. Astronomers think that, billions of years ago, Uranus was knocked sideways by a collision with another planet.

Uranus's orbit takes 84 years. The planet's north pole has 42 years of sunlight, followed by 42 years of darkness.

Cold Planet

Uranus is not the farthest planet from the Sun, but it is the coldest. Its surface reaches –224 °C (–371 °F), a few degrees colder than Neptune. This is also a result of Uranus's collision, which let out some of the heat trapped inside the planet.

Lights, known as auroras, can be seen near Uranus's icy surface. They are made when gases are lit up by particles from the Sun.

Uranus's dark rings may be pieces of shattered moons.

The 13 rings are no more than 600 million years old.

URANUS
SIZE: 51,118 km (31,763 miles) across
DISTANCE FROM THE SUN:
  2.9 billion km (1.8 billion miles)
KNOWN MOONS: 27

Uranus   Earth

NEPTUNE

As the most distant planet from the Sun, Neptune has the longest orbit. The planet spends 165 years on its journey around the Sun, covering 28.3 billion km (17.6 billion miles).

The Great Dark Spot was a storm seen by the *Voyager 2* space probe in 1989.

Going the Wrong Way!

Neptune's largest moon is named Triton. The Solar System's other large moons orbit their planet in the same direction the planet is rotating. Triton goes the other way! Astronomers think this is because Triton did not form at the same time as Neptune, but was a dwarf planet tugged by Neptune's gravity.

Triton is 2,710 km (1,680 miles) wide.

NEPTUNE

PROTEUS

TRITON

Beyond Neptune

At least four dwarf planets orbit beyond Neptune. From largest to smallest, they are: Pluto, Eris, Haumea, and Makemake. Pluto's orbit is stretched and tilted, so sometimes it travels closer to the Sun than Neptune.

Around 2,376 km (1,476 miles) wide, the dwarf planet Pluto has five moons.

These white streaks are clouds of frozen methane.

NEPTUNE

SIZE: 49,528 km (30,775 miles) across
DISTANCE FROM THE SUN: 4.5 billion km
    (2.8 billion miles)
KNOWN MOONS: 14

Neptune   Earth

THE UNIVERSE

The Universe is more than 93 billion light years across. That means it would take more than 93 billion years for a beam of light to travel across it, past stars, galaxies, and vast areas of emptiness. Yet the Universe is still growing!

UNIVERSE

LOCAL GROUP CLUSTER

Shining Stars

A star is a ball of gas, mostly hydrogen and helium. In a star's tightly squeezed core, tiny particles of hydrogen, called atoms, are constantly crashing together. As they crash, the hydrogen atoms join together to make helium atoms—and release lots of energy.

Energy travels from a star's core to its surface—and into space. On Earth, we see and feel that energy as light and heat.

Our galaxy is one of around 80 galaxies in our Local Group cluster.

SOLAR SYSTEM

28

Grouping Galaxies

Stars are grouped into galaxies. These are collections of stars, planets, gas, and dust which are held together by gravity, the force that pulls all objects toward each other. Several galaxies usually group into clusters, which group into superclusters.

Around 160 million light years from Earth, these four galaxies, known as Robert's Quartet, are held together by gravity.

MILKY WAY GALAXY

THE VISIBLE UNIVERSE
SIZE: 93 billion light years across
AGE: 13.8 billion years
NUMBER OF GALAXY
   SUPERCLUSTERS: Around 10 million

EARTH

MOON

Our Solar System is one of billions of solar systems in our galaxy.

29

TYPES OF STAR

Stars are all different sizes, some much smaller than our Sun and others much more massive! Our Sun is an average-size, average-hot star known as a yellow dwarf.

Never look at the Sun, as its brightness will hurt your eyes.

Blue, Yellow, Red ...

The most massive stars are usually the hottest and brightest. The hottest stars give off blue light. Cooler stars shine yellow or—if they are cooler still—red. Smaller stars are named dwarfs, while bigger ones are giants or supergiants.

The biggest supergiants are 2.4 billion km (1.5 billion miles) across.

RED DWARF: TRAPPIST-1

YELLOW DWARF: THE SUN

RED GIANT: ALDEBARAN

BLUE SUPERGIANT: RIGEL

The Sun gives off flares, which are bursts of light.

Nearest Star

The nearest star to the Sun is Proxima Centauri, which is 4.2 light years away. Its name means "nearest of Centaurus," as it can be seen—using a telescope, as it is very faint—in the constellation of Centaurus. It is a red dwarf, only 214,550 km (133,315 miles) wide.

This illustration shows Proxima Centauri (glowing red near the middle) alongside its nearest stars, Alpha Centauri A and B (bottom right). In the distance is our yellow Sun.

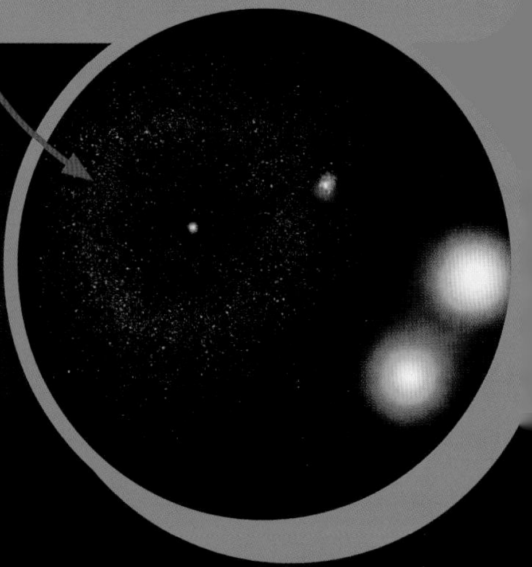

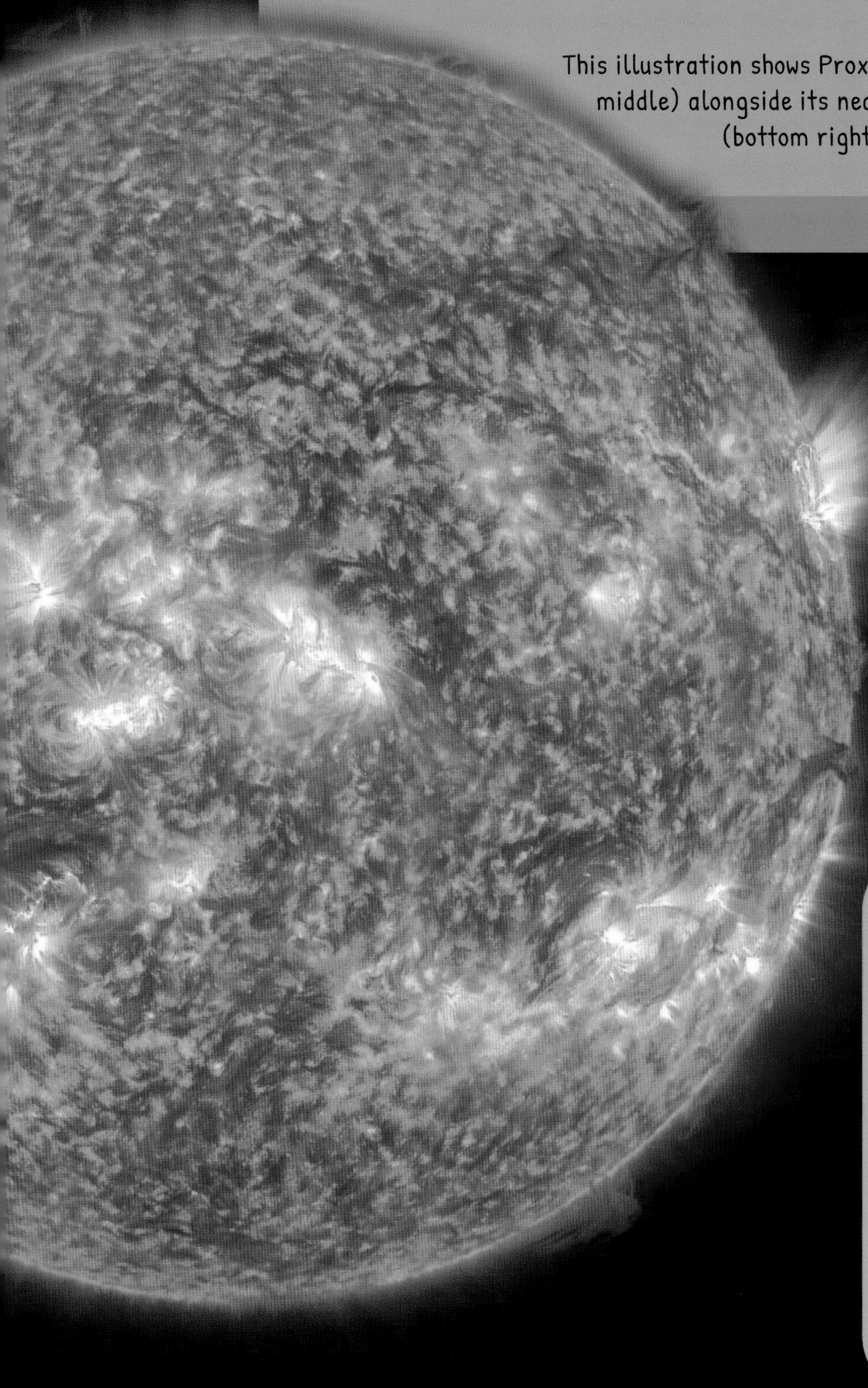

THE SUN
SIZE: 1.4 million km (0.86 million miles) across
AGE: 4.6 billion years
SURFACE TEMPERATURE: 6,000 °C (10,800 °F)

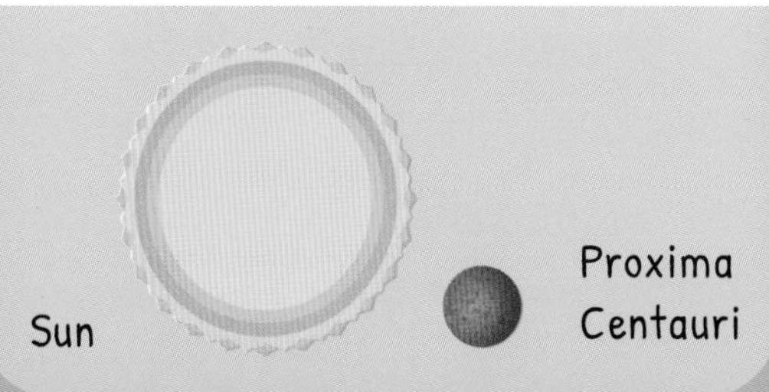

Sun

Proxima Centauri

STAR BIRTH

Our Sun was born around 4.6 billion years ago, which makes it a middle-aged star! Astronomers think that around 400 million new stars are born every day.

Around 5 light years long, this cloud is a star nursery.

AP COLUMBAE
SIZE: 532,000 km
    (330,000 miles) across
AGE: 40 million years
DISTANCE FROM EARTH:
    27 light years

AP Columbae   Sun

Starting Out

A new star is usually born in a thick cloud of dust and gas. A clump forms in the cloud, its gravity pulling more dust and gas toward it. At last, the ball gets so hot and dense that hydrogen atoms crash together in its core—and a glowing star is born!

Named the Pillars of Creation, this nursery is 7,000 light years from Earth.

A very young star, known as a protostar, is still gathering dust and gas from its cloud.

Star Nurseries

Stars usually form in thick clouds named stellar nurseries (stellar means "star"). However, the closest young star to Earth, AP Columbae, is not in a nursery. It formed when a star exploded, shooting out gas and dust that made new stars!

W51 is one of the biggest star nurseries in the Milky Way.

STAR DEATH

When a star runs out of hydrogen and other fuel, it starts to die. Every star will die eventually. Our Sun will run out of hydrogen in around 5 billion years—long after humans have found somewhere else to live!

the Crab Nebula is a supernova remnant.

How Small Stars Die

When a Sun-sized star runs out of fuel, it swells into a red giant. It throws out gas, making a glowing cloud known as a planetary nebula. Then the star shrinks into a faint white dwarf.

Over billions of years, a white dwarf will stop giving out light, becoming a black dwarf. The Universe is too young for there to be any black dwarfs yet.

SUN-SIZED STAR

RED

PLANETARY

WHITE

BLACK DWARF

MASSIVE STAR

BLACK HOLE

RED SUPERGIANT

SUPERNOVA

NEUTRON STAR

How Big Stars Die

When a star more than 10 times bigger than the Sun runs out of fuel, it swells into a supergiant. Then it explodes, known as a supernova. A cloud of gas and dust, known as a supernova remnant, is blown out. The explosion leaves behind a neutron star or—for stars more than 20 times bigger than the Sun— a black hole (see page 36).

A supernova leaves a tiny, very dense neutron star or an even tinier, even denser black hole.

CRAB NEBULA
SIZE: 11 light years across
AGE: 1,000 years
DISTANCE FROM EARTH:
6,500 light years

Crab Nebula

Solar System

At its heart is a neutron star 20 km (12 miles) across.

BLACK HOLES

A black hole is an area of space with such strong gravity that nothing can escape its pull. It can suck in stars and planets! A black hole can form when a massive star explodes.

This illustration shows the hot dust and gas swirling around a black hole.

SUPERMASSIVE BLACK HOLE M87*
SIZE: 38 billion km (23.6 billion miles) across
MASS: 6 billion Suns
DISTANCE FROM EARTH: 55 million light years

M87*   Solar System

A black hole looks black because it sucks in light.

Great Gravity!

The bigger an object's mass (how heavy it is), the stronger the pull of its gravity. When a black hole is formed by the death of a massive star, the black hole has a mass up to 100 times our Sun's. All that mass is packed into an area the size of a city. The strength of a black hole's gravity can deform space.

Within an area called the "event horizon," dust, gas, and stars are sucked into a black hole.

Supermassive Black Holes

There is a supermassive black hole in the middle of most galaxies, including our own. Supermassive black holes have a mass millions of times our Sun's. They may form when ordinary black holes grow by sucking in material or when several stars explode at once.

This was the first photo of a black hole ever taken, in 2019. It shows the supermassive black hole in galaxy M87, surrounded by glowing gas.

37

TYPES OF GALAXY

The smallest galaxies have only a thousand stars, but the biggest have 100 trillion (1 followed by 14 zeros). Smaller galaxies, known as dwarfs, orbit around larger galaxies, known as giants and supergiants.

The Southern Pinwheel Galaxy has a bright central bar.

SOUTHERN PINWHEEL GALAXY
SIZE: 55,000 light years across
NUMBER OF STARS: 40 billion
DISTANCE FROM EARTH: 15 million light years

Southern Pinwheel

Milky Way

This galaxy is a spiral galaxy, with arms of dense gas, dust, and stars.

Spiral galaxies have a bright central bulge (shown here) or central bar.

Three Shapes

Galaxies have three main shapes: spiral, elliptical, and irregular. Spiral galaxies have curving arms that turn around the galaxy's bright middle. Elliptical galaxies are often the shape of a flattened ball. Irregular galaxies have no definite shape.

Elliptical galaxies may form when galaxies join together.

Irregular galaxies may have been pulled out of shape by a bigger galaxy.

Pulling a Porpoise

When galaxies are a few hundred thousand light years apart, they can be pulled out of shape by each other's gravity. The Porpoise Galaxy used to be a spiral galaxy, but it has been pulled by an elliptical galaxy.

The Porpoise Galaxy has the shape of a porpoise, a dolphin-like sea animal!

THE MILKY WAY

Our galaxy, named the Milky Way, has around 100 billion stars. That's a lot—if you visited one star per second it would take you 3,100 years to reach them all. The Milky Way is is a spiral galaxy with a bar of bright, old stars at its middle.

Getting a Picture

Since our planet is inside the Milky Way's disk, it is difficult to understand the galaxy's shape. It was only in 2019 that telescope photos proved the galaxy has a bar at its middle. Until a spacecraft leaves the galaxy, we will be able to "see" its whole shape only in illustrations.

In the night sky, the edge of the galaxy can be seen as a pale, milky stripe of stars and dust, earning it the name Milky Way.

A supermassive black hole is in our galaxy's central bar.

Hangers On

Around 50 smaller galaxies orbit the Milky Way. They are known as satellite galaxies. The largest is the Large Magellanic Cloud, around 160,000 light years away. It is a dwarf galaxy with a smudged spiral shape due to the pull of our galaxy.

In this photo of the sky over Indonesia, we can see the Large Magellanic Cloud (on the lower left) and a smaller satellite, the Small Magellanic Cloud (above and to the right).

The galaxy's arms turn at a speed of around 210 km (130 miles) per second.

THE MILKY WAY
SIZE: 105,700 light years across
MASS: 1.5 trillion Suns
AGE: 13.6 billion years

Milky Way

Large Magellanic Cloud

EXOPLANETS

Exoplanets are planets outside our Solar System. Astronomers have discovered 5,000 exoplanets so far, but they think there are quintillions more in orbit around stars across the Universe.

Nearest Exoplanet

Our nearest exoplanets orbit our nearest star, Proxima Centauri. The two planets are named Proxima b and Proxima c. Proxima b was discovered in 2016, while its sister planet was spotted three years later.

Astronomers think Proxima b has a rocky surface.

Proxima b might look a little like Mars.

PROXIMA B

SIZE: Possibly around 14,000 km (8,700 miles) across
AGE: Around 4.8 billion years
DISTANCE FROM EARTH: 4.2 light years

Proxima b

Earth

Proxima Centauri, and Alpha Centauri A and B, shine in the sky.

TOO HOT

TOO COLD

JUST RIGHT

Is There Life?

Astronomers study exoplanets to see if they are suitable for living things. For living things to exist, an exoplanet must be the right distance from its star. Proxima b is one of many exoplanets that might be suitable, but no signs of life have been spotted!

If a planet is the right temperature, it might have flowing water. All known living things need water.

43

QUASARS

A quasar is a galaxy with a very bright supermassive black hole. As the black hole sucks in dust, gas, and stars, jets of light are thrown out. A quasar shines with the brightness of trillions of Suns.

This illustration shows a double quasar 10 billion light years away.

A quasar points a little away from Earth.

A blazar points at Earth, making it one of the brightest objects in the Universe.

Active Galaxies

Quasars are known as active galaxies because they have a very active black hole. Blazars are another type of active galaxy. Actually, astronomers think all active galaxies are the same, but we just see them differently, depending on whether their jet is pointing at Earth.

Young and Busy

All quasars are at least 600 million light years from Earth. The Milky Way and other nearby galaxies have quiet black holes. The light from galaxies farther from Earth has taken a long time to reach us, so we see the galaxies as they were when they were young. Young galaxies have more active black holes.

Quasar PG 0052+251 is 1.4 billion light years from Earth, in a spiral galaxy. It was photographed by the Hubble Space Telescope.

QUASAR PG 0052+251
SIZE: Around 1.5 light years across
MASS OF BLACK HOLE: 360 million Suns
AGE: Probably less than 1 billion years

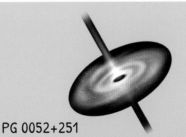

PG 0052+251   ● Solar System

Double quasars are found where two active galaxies are joining together.

GALAXY CLUSTERS

Galaxies are often found in clusters. Our galaxy is in the Local Group galaxy cluster, which is in the Virgo Supercluster, part of the even bigger Laniakea Supercluster. This supercluster is part of a galaxy filament known as the Pisces-Cetus Supercluster Complex.

Andromeda is the largest galaxy in the Local Group.

LANIAKEA SUPERCLUSTER
SIZE: 520 million light years across
MASS: 100 quadrillion Suns (1 followed by 17 zeros)
NUMBER OF GALAXIES: 100,000

The Local Group

Our galaxy cluster contains at least 80 galaxies. The cluster is around 10 million light years across. The three largest galaxies in the cluster are spirals: Andromeda, the Milky Way, and Triangulum.

The Local Group contains the Milky Way and its satellites (lower left), as well as Andromeda and its satellites.

Around 2.5 million light years away, it is 220,000 light years across.

Galaxy Filaments

Galaxy filaments are the largest structures in the Universe. They are made up of galaxy superclusters. Our galaxy filament is 1 billion light years long and 150 million light years wide.

This illustration shows how filaments link together, forming a web. Between the filaments are voids, which contain very few galaxies.

THE BIG BANG

The Universe began 13.8 billion years ago with what astronomers have named the Big Bang. In that first moment, the Universe started to grow from a tiny, very hot point. After 100 million years, the first stars were born.

200 MILLION YEAR

100 MILLION YEARS

300,000 YEARS

Atoms start to form. They are the building blocks for stars and people.

THE BIG BANG
WHEN: 13.8 billion years ago
SIZE OF UNIVERSE AFTER 1 SECOND:
   Around 18 light years across
TEMPERATURE OF UNIVERSE AFTER 1 SECOND:
   1 quadrillion °C (1.8 quadrillion °F)

Growing, Growing ...

The Universe has never stopped growing. Today, it does not grow as quickly as it did in the first moments. Yet galaxies are still getting farther and farther away from each other.

It is easiest to understand the Universe's growth if we imagine it is a balloon that is being blown up. Galaxies are like dots drawn on the balloon.

The first galaxies start to form after around 200 million years.

Moving Away

The farther away from us a galaxy is, the faster it seems to be moving away. Imagine you are one of the dots on the balloon above. As the balloon expands, the dots close to you do not seem to move very much, but the distant dots seem to move much farther!

The galaxy NGC 7513 is 62 million light years from Earth. It is moving away from us by 1,564 km (972 miles) per second.

49

WATCHING THE SKY

We can watch the night sky with our bare eyes or—to see more distant objects—with binoculars or a telescope. The most powerful telescopes on Earth have the power of 4 million human eyes!

How Telescopes Work

We can see stars and galaxies because they give off light, which enters our eyes. Telescopes use mirrors to gather more light than human eyes can collect. Telescopes also use curved pieces of glass, known as lenses, to magnify images (make them bigger), so that distant objects become clearer.

In a reflecting telescope, the curving primary mirror collects lots of light.

LENS

SECONDARY MIRROR

LIGHT

PRIMARY MIRROR

With our bare eyes, we can see stars up to 4,000 light years away.

Biggest Telescope

The biggest single-mirrored telescope on Earth is the Gran Telescopio Canarias, in Spain. It is powerful enough to study black holes and planets orbiting distant stars.

Like other large telescopes, the Gran Telescopio Canarias is on a mountaintop, where its view is not spoiled by bad weather, pollution, and light from cities.

A store-bought telescope reveals galaxies millions of light years away.

GRAN TELESCOPIO CANARIAS
SIZE OF PRIMARY MIRROR:
   10.4 m (34.1 ft) across
IN ACTION: From 2007
EQUIPMENT: Mirrors for gathering light, as well as instruments for collecting infrared energy

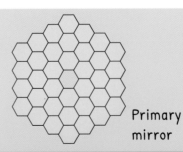

Primary mirror

CONSTELLATIONS

Constellations are groups of stars that form a pattern in the night sky. The stars in a constellation are often many light years apart, but they look close together when seen from Earth!

The bright star Sirius is in the Canis Major ("Greater Dog") constellation.

Northern Constellations

Astronomers agree on 88 constellations. More than half of them can be seen from north of the equator during some or all of the year. The ancient Greeks named 48 of these constellations after people and animals from their myths.

This 19th-century star map shows the constellation Perseus, named after a Greek hero who cut the head off a monster.

The Orion constellation can be spotted by the three stars in the hunter's belt.

Southern Constellations

Many of the southern constellations were given their official names after the 16th century. Some are named after scientific instruments, such as a microscope (Microscopium) or telescope (Telescopium).

Microscopium (left) and Telescopium (right) are on either side of Sagittarius, who was a mythological centaur with the upper body of a human and the legs of a horse.

ORION CONSTELLATION
DISTANCE OF NEAREST STAR
FROM EARTH: 245 light years
CAN BE SEEN: Across the world
NAMED AFTER: A hunter in Greek
mythology who had a dog named Sirius

POLE STARS

As Earth turns around its axis, the stars seem to rotate around us—even though it is us moving, not them! Only the stars above the north and south poles seem to stay still. Knowing how to find the pole stars is useful for finding our way at night.

The other stars seem to rotate around the North Star.

North Pole Star

The North Star is the brightest star in the constellation of Ursa Minor ("Little Bear"). Although it looks like a single star, it is actually three stars orbiting each other, around 433 light years away.

To find the North Star and know which direction is north, follow a line from the "big dipper" (or "plough") shape in the nearby constellation of Ursa Major ("Great Bear").

URSA MINOR

NORTH STAR

BIG DIPPER

South Pole Star

The South Star is a faint star in the constellation of Octans. It is a single, giant star around 294 light years from Earth.

The South Star is just outside the triangle of Octans, which is named after a measuring instrument: the octant.

OCTANS

SOUTH STAR

If many photos are taken during one night, they can be combined to show star trails.

URSA MAJOR CONSTELLATION
DISTANCE OF NEAREST STAR FROM EARTH: 8 light years
CAN BE SEEN: From most of the northern hemisphere
NAMED AFTER: A mother bear in Greek mythology

THE PLANETS

The closest planets—Mercury, Venus, Mars, Jupiter, and Saturn—can be seen as lights in the night sky during some of the year. Unlike stars, the planets do not produce their own light: The light we see is reflected sunlight.

VENUS

JUPITER

MARS

When two or more planets look close together, it is called a conjunction.

No Twinkling

Stars seem to twinkle because of the distance their light has journeyed to reach our eyes. Since planets are much closer, they do not appear to twinkle.

Due to its red dust, Mars (pictured) glows red. The other planets glow whitish or yellowish.

Venus is the brightest planet in the night sky.

MERCURY

HOW OFTEN: When the planet is farthest from the Sun, as seen from Earth

HOW LONG: Since Mercury is the closest planet to the Sun, it can be seen only in the hour before sunrise or in the hour after sunset

WHERE TO SEE: Close to the horizon

Where to Look

The planets can be seen along the ecliptic, an imaginary curving line that the Sun seems to travel along over the course of the day. Since all the planets (and the Moon) orbit the Sun in the same plane—as if they are circling it on a dinner plate—the planets seem to move along the ecliptic, too.

This picture combines lots of photos, taken 6 minutes apart over one night and morning. It shows (from left to right), the journeys of the Sun, Venus, the Moon, and Jupiter along the ecliptic as we look toward the middle of our Solar System's "dinner plate" while Earth turns.

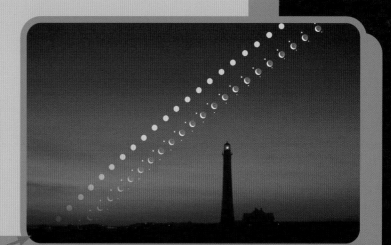

ECLIPSES

An eclipse is when a planet, moon, or star is hidden for a few moments, either because another object passes in front or because it moves into the shadow of another object. We can see eclipses of the Sun and Moon every few years.

Eclipses of the Sun

An eclipse of the Sun happens when the Moon passes between Earth and the Sun, hiding the Sun. It can happen only when the Sun, Moon, and Earth are in a perfectly straight line.

A total eclipse of the Sun can be seen around once every 18 months from somewhere on Earth.

MOON

EARTH

SUN

TOTAL ECLIPSE

PARTIAL ECLIPSE

This step-by-step picture shows the Moon crossing the Sun.

Even during a total eclipse, never look directly at the Sun!

Eclipses of the Moon

A total eclipse of the Moon is when the Earth is between the Sun and the Moon, with the three lined up so the Moon is completely in Earth's shadow.

We can still see the Moon during a total eclipse because it is lit by sunlight that has been bent by Earth's atmosphere. This light makes the Moon look red.

TOTAL ECLIPSE OF THE MOON
HOW OFTEN: At least twice every 3 years
HOW LONG: Up to 2 hours
WHERE TO SEE: On the night side of Earth

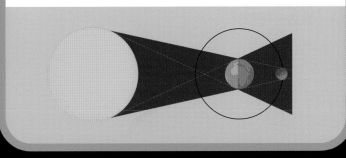

TRANSITS

A transit is when a smaller object moves in front of a bigger object. The smaller object does not block our view of the bigger one, but seems to move across its face.

This photo of the Moon transiting Earth was taken by a satellite.

TITAN TRANSITING SATURN

HOW OFTEN: Saturn's largest moon will transit several times in 2025, then not until 2038

HOW LONG: Up to 5 hours

WHERE TO SEE: On the night side of Earth with a good telescope

We can see the Moon's far side, which is never visible from Earth.

Transits of the Sun

From Earth, we can see the planets that are closer to the Sun—Mercury and Venus—move across the face of the Sun. Mercury transits the Sun 13 or 14 times in every century. Venus last crossed the Sun's face in 2012 and will not do so again until 2117.

It takes Venus around 6 hours to cross the Sun's face. Remember: Never look directly at the Sun!

Transits of Jupiter

With a good telescope, we can watch Jupiter's four largest moons—or their shadows—cross the planet's face. Transits of a single moon happen many times a year. The four moons never transit together.

The shadows of three of Jupiter's moons cross its face together only twice in every 10 years.

CALLISTO'S SHADOW

GANYMEDE

GANYMEDE'S SHADOW

IO'S SHADOW

IO

SUPERMOONS

The Moon's orbit around Earth is not quite circular. This means it is sometimes nearer to Earth than at other times. When the Moon is closer to Earth and fully lit by sunlight, it looks bigger than usual—this is a supermoon.

Nearest and Farthest

When the Moon is closest to Earth (named its perigee), it is 362,600 km (225,309 miles) away. When it is farthest from Earth (named its apogee), it is 405,400 km (251,904 miles) away.

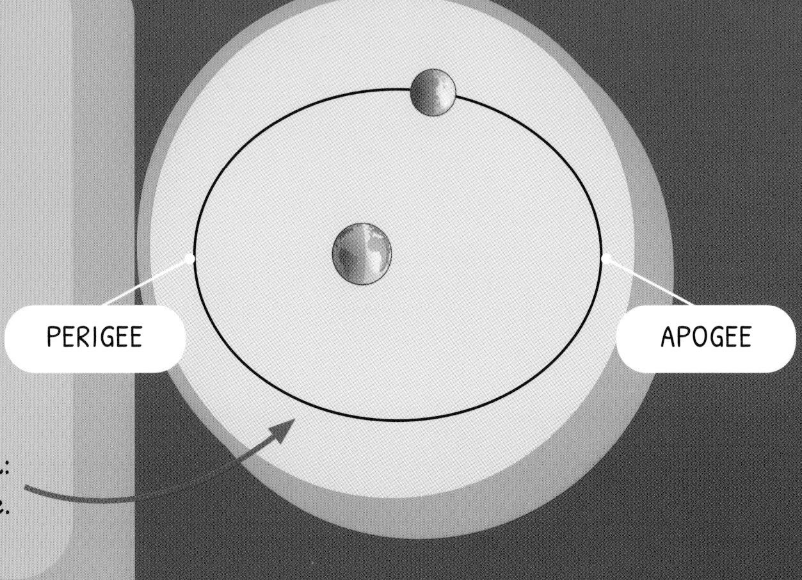

The Moon's orbit is elliptical: a slightly stretched-out circle.

PERIGEE

APOGEE

A supermoon reflects more sunlight, giving us brighter "moonlight."

A supermoon rises over Washington DC, in the United States.

MICROMOON: FULL MOON AT APOGEE

SUPERMOON: FULL MOON AT PERIGEE

Supermoon Times

The Moon is at its perigee once in every orbit, but not always when the Moon is full (completely lit by the Sun). Once in every 14 orbits, the Moon is at its perigee while full, but the Full Moons on either side are only a little smaller, so there are usually between two and five supermoons in a row.

When the Full Moon is at perigee, its area is 25 percent (a quarter) bigger than when it is at apogee.

SUPERMOONS

HOW OFTEN: Two to five times a year
HOW LONG: One night
WHERE TO SEE: On the night side of Earth

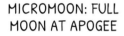

Supermoon and Earth to scale

EQUINOXES

The tilt of Earth's axis means the Sun is not usually exactly over the equator. In fact, there are only two days a year when the the middle of the Sun is directly above the equator. These days are the equinoxes, and they occur in March and September.

The June solstice is the northern hemisphere's longest day.

Terrific Tilt

On the equinoxes, the Earth's tilt is neither toward nor away from the Sun. Midway between the equinoxes are the solstices, when Earth's axis points most dramatically toward or away from the Sun.

The solstices are in June and December of every year.

JUNE SOLSTICE

EQUATOR

DECEMBER SOLSTICE

MARCH AND SEPTEMBER EQUINOXES

This photo shows the Sun's path on the December solstice in the northern hemisphere. The Sun rises late and sets early, never rising high in the sky.

Changing Days

On the equinoxes, day and night are of nearly equal length everywhere on Earth. In contrast, the December solstice is the shortest day of the year in the northern hemisphere and the longest day in the southern hemisphere. The June solstice is the opposite way around.

People celebrate the sunrise at England's ancient Stonehenge.

EQUINOXES
HOW OFTEN: Twice a year, around March 22 and September 23
HOW LONG: One day
WHERE TO SEE: Everywhere on Earth

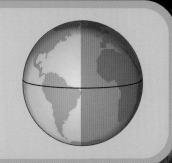

COMETS

A comet is an icy ball of dust and rock which orbits the Sun. Yet its orbit is so stretched and long that it travels both close to and very far from the Sun. When a comet nears the Sun, it heats up—and may be seen as a bright streak in the sky.

Growing Tails

As a comet moves inside Mars's orbit around the Sun, it gets hot enough to release gas, which can be seen as a streaming, glowing tail. As a comet nears the Sun, a second tail grows, made of dust.

A comet's gas tail is always blown away from the Sun.

COMET'S ORBIT

GAS TAIL

DUST TAIL

EARTH'S ORBIT

COMET HALLEY

HOW OFTEN: Last seen in 1986,
  it will reappear in 2061
HOW LONG: A few days
WHERE TO SEE: Away from city lights

The comet's gas tail stretched for millions of miles.

Comet Neowise was seen from Earth in 2020 and will reappear in 6,800 years.

Long and Short

Comet Encke has the shortest orbit around the Sun: 3.3 years. The comet with the longest known orbit is Comet West, which journeys for at least 254,000 years. However, there may be comets with much longer orbits that we have not spotted!

Comet Halley has an orbit of 75-76 years. Shortly after it was seen in 1066, the comet was stitched into the famous Bayeux Tapestry.

ISTI MIRANT STELLA

METEOR SHOWERS

During a meteor shower, many streaks of light can be seen in the night sky. These streaks, known as meteors or shooting stars, are made as little space rocks burn up in Earth's atmosphere.

The Perseid meteor shower is caused by Comet Swift–Tuttle's tail.

Making Meteors

Meteors are made by rock or metal dust and chunks, known as meteoroids. These are usually bits of comets or asteroids. As the meteoroids zoom through the atmosphere, they push against the air, which makes them really hot.

Most meteoroids are so small that they burn up completely in the air.

Comet dust burns as it falls through the air.

Mighty Meteorites

Meteor showers are usually caused by specks of comet dust, which burn up before they reach the ground. Bigger meteoroids—which do not burn up fully—are usually chunks of asteroid. When a meteoroid reaches the ground, it is named a meteorite.

Every year, around 6,000 meteorites land on Earth. Most are small and fall unnoticed in the ocean or desert.

PERSEID METEOR SHOWER
HOW OFTEN: Every year, when Earth's orbit goes through Swift-Tuttle's dust cloud
HOW LONG: Mid-July to late August
WHERE TO SEE: Streaking from near the Perseus constellation

AURORAS

Auroras are patterns of light that shimmer and spiral in the sky. They can be seen mostly around Earth's north pole, where they are often called the "northern lights," or around the south pole, where they are known as the "southern lights."

Green auroras are the most commonly seen.

Excited Gases

The Sun releases particles that carry lots of energy. When the particles meet gases in Earth's atmosphere, the gases become excited—and shine. Due to its iron core, Earth is a huge magnet. The Sun's particles are attracted to the magnet's poles.

Due to Earth's magnetism, auroras are usually seen around the poles.

ENERGY-CARRYING PARTICLES

SUN

EARTH'S

Green, Blue, or Red?

Earth's atmosphere is mostly nitrogen and oxygen gas. When nitrogen gets excited, it gives off blue or purple light. When oxygen is excited, it usually glows green.

Red auroras are the rarest, as they happen only when oxygen high in the atmosphere is excited by a very intense stream of particles from the Sun.

Auroras can be watched in Norway during the winter.

NORTHERN LIGHTS

HOW OFTEN: All year, but best seen on cloudless nights between September and March

HOW LONG: Between nightfall and sunrise

WHERE TO SEE: In a band around Earth's far north, far from city lights

MISSIONS TO SPACE

Astronomers say that space begins 100 km (62 miles) above Earth's surface. A rocket was the first human-made object to enter space, in 1949. It was another 12 years before a human reached space.

American astronaut Mae Jemison orbited Earth 127 times.

Brave Astronauts

In 1961, the first human in space was the Soviet Union's Yuri Gagarin. Since then, more than 500 people have visited space. Most of them have been highly trained astronauts, but since 2001 a few have been space tourists, who paid for their trip.

Yuri Gagarin is strapped into his Vostok 3KA space capsule, before blasting off to make one orbit around Earth.

Jemison flew on board Space Shuttle *Endeavour* in 1992.

Where Have Humans Been?

Humans have orbited Earth and the Moon many times, but the Moon is the only place apart from Earth where humans have set foot. However, uncrewed spacecraft have landed on—or deliberately crashed into—Mercury, Venus, Mars, Jupiter, Saturn and its moon Titan, and a few asteroids and comets.

Saturn has no solid surface to land on, but the *Cassini* spacecraft flew into the planet's atmosphere, where it managed to send home information before it was destroyed.

VOSTOK 3KA
SIZE: 4.6 m (15 ft) long and 2.4 m (7.9 ft) wide
IN ACTION: 1961–63
EQUIPMENT: Braking engine and escape system

73

ROCKETS

All spacecraft are lifted into space by a rocket. Once a rocket has done its work, it separates from its spacecraft—and either stays in space or falls to Earth, where it lands harmlessly in the ocean.

A Russian Soyuz-2 rocket lifts off from Kazakhstan.

Up, Up, and Away

To beat the pull of Earth's gravity, a rocket must reach a speed of 40,000 km (25,000 miles) an hour. To do this, a rocket needs lots of fuel, which is burnt in its engines to release a blast of gas. By blasting the gas downward, the rocket shoots upward—like kicking water backward makes you swim forward!

A rocket has nozzles through which it blasts hot gas.

In Stages

Rockets have between two and five parts, named stages, each with its own engines and fuel. When a rocket takes off, only its first stage fires its engine. When that stage has burned its fuel, it is dropped. The next stage takes over, then is dropped ... The remaining rocket weighs less and less, so it can fly faster.

This illustration shows the inside (left) and outside of the Saturn V rocket, which lifted all the human missions to the Moon.

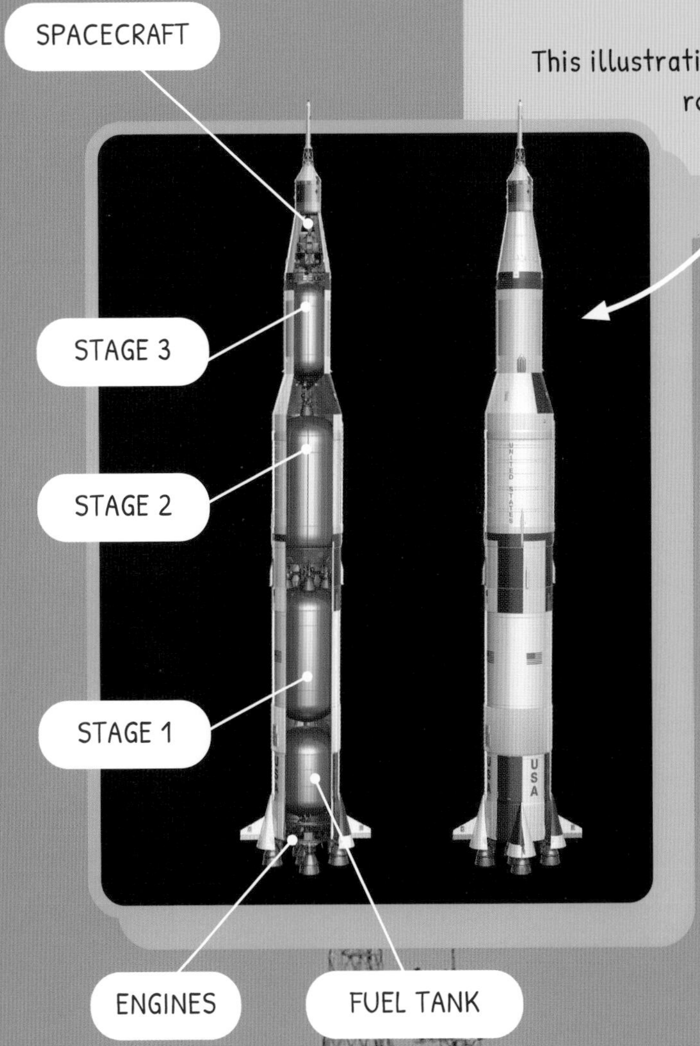

SPACECRAFT

STAGE 3

STAGE 2

STAGE 1

ENGINES

FUEL TANK

SOYUZ-2
SIZE: 46.3 m (152 ft) tall and 2.95 m (9.7 ft) wide
IN ACTION: From 2004
EQUIPMENT: two stages for low orbits or three stages for higher orbits

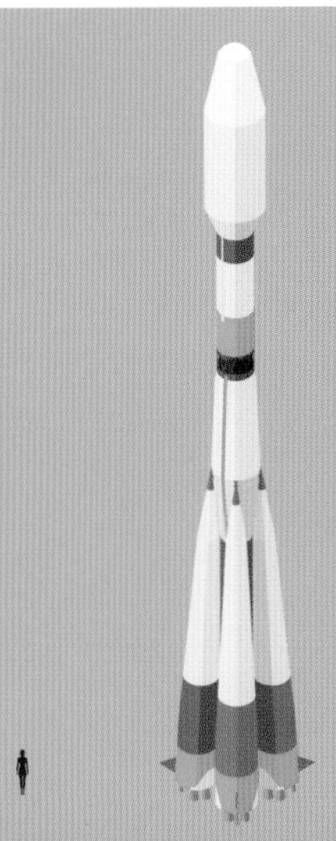

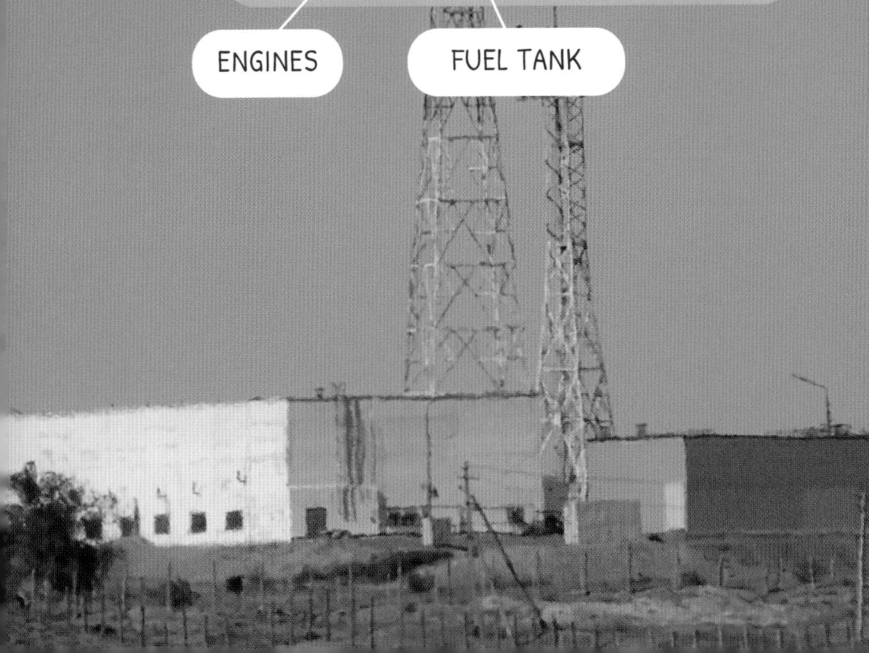

SPACE CAPSULES

Most spacecraft that have carried humans have been space capsules. While in space, a space capsule is steered using its engines, which blast in different directions. But a space capsule has no wings, so—once it has completed its mission—it falls to Earth!

Neil Armstrong took this photo of Buzz Aldrin on the Moon.

Falling Down

A space capsule's fall through Earth's atmosphere is slowed by a parachute or backward-blasting engines. It lands in the ocean or desert. Although the crew is cushioned, most space capsules are designed to be used only once, as they are damaged by the impact.

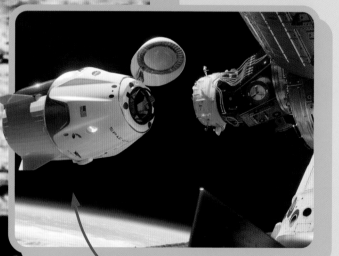

Launched in 2020, Crew Dragon 2 is a space capsule that carries crew to the International Space Station.

Armstrong and the lunar module are reflected in Aldrin's helmet.

APOLLO COMMAND MODULE
SIZE: 3.2 m (10.6 ft) tall and 3.9 m (12.8 ft) wide
IN ACTION: 1966–75
EQUIPMENT: Seats, food, water, engines, parachutes, and around 700 controls and displays

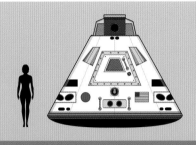

Walking on the Moon

The first humans on the Moon were US astronauts Neil Armstrong and Edwin "Buzz" Aldrin, in 1969. Their Apollo space capsule had three parts: the command module, which was the cabin and the only part that returned to Earth; the service module, which held the engine; and the lunar module.

LUNAR MODULE

The lunar module flew to the Moon's surface while the command and service modules, along with astronaut Michael Collins, remained in orbit around the Moon.

COMMAND MODULE

SERVICE MODULE

SPACEPLANES

Unlike space capsules, spaceplanes have wings, so they can fly down to Earth then land like an ordinary plane. This means they can be re-used. Despite this benefit, there have not been many spaceplanes—so far!

Space Shuttle

The most successful spaceplanes were the United States' five Space Shuttles, which flew 135 missions before they were retired in 2011. They carried crew to the International Space Station and positioned satellites in orbit around Earth.

To lift off, a Space Shuttle fired its engines, which used fuel from a large orange fuel tank, and got extra power from two white booster rockets. The tank and boosters were dropped after launch.

A Space Shuttle weighed 75,000 kg (165,000 lb) when empty.

A total of 355 astronauts flew on Space Shuttles.

Melting Heat

As spaceplanes re-enter Earth's atmosphere, they must not melt in the 1,650 °C (3,000 °F) heat as they push against the air. They have a heatproof coating, which makes them heavy and expensive to fly—and explains why there have not been many spaceplanes!

A new spaceplane, named Dream Chaser, is a quarter of the length of the old Space Shuttles, making it much lighter.

SPACE SHUTTLE
SIZE: 37 m (121 ft) long and 23.8 m (78 ft) wingspan
IN ACTION: 1981–2011
EQUIPMENT: three main rocket engines, kitchen, bathroom, seats, bunks, work areas, and 2,214 controls and displays

SATELLITES

A human-made satellite is a machine that is placed in orbit around Earth—or another planet or moon. The first satellite, the Soviet Union's *Sputnik 1*, went into orbit in 1957. Today, there are at least 5,000 satellites orbiting our planet.

Landsat 9 takes photos of Earth's forests and cities to see how they change.

What Do They Do?

Some satellites orbiting Earth are watching the weather or taking photos of sea ice or wildfires. Others are communications satellites, which bounce TV, phone, and internet signals around the world. Many satellites are used for navigation (finding the way).

If a car "satnav" (satellite navigation device) receives signals from three navigation satellites, it knows how far away each satellite is and can calculate where it is.

Why Don't They Fall?

Satellites are pulled toward Earth by its gravity, but at the same time they are speeding along at more than 10,000 km (6,000 miles) per hour. This means that their fall is curved so they circle Earth rather than dropping onto it.

A satellite gains its speed from the rocket that lifted it into space. Without anything to slow the satellite down, it carries on moving at the same speed—which makes it orbit.

Satellite speeds in this direction.

Gravity pulls toward Earth.

A solar panel turns sunlight into electricity to power the cameras.

LANDSAT 9
SIZE: 3 m (9.8 ft) long and 4.6 m (15 ft) wide
IN ACTION: From 2021
EQUIPMENT: Cameras that take photos and also reveal the temperatures of Earth's surface

INTERNATIONAL SPACE STATION

The International Space Station (ISS) is a huge satellite where astronauts live and work for months at a time. It orbits 400 km (250 miles) above Earth. The space station was put together in orbit, section by section, by astronauts.

Falling and Floating

Astronauts float around inside the ISS. This is because the ISS experiences microgravity, where people and objects appear to be weightless. As Earth's gravity pulls on the ISS and its astronauts, both the people and the space station fall toward Earth (but it is a curving, never-ending fall; see page 81). As everything falls together, people appear to float!

see page 81

Microgravity does not mean there is no gravity, just that gravity appears to have little effect!

INTERNATIONAL SPACE STATION

SIZE: 109 m (358 ft) long and
      73 m (239 ft) wide
IN ACTION: From 1998
EQUIPMENT: Areas for working, sleeping,
      exercising, cooking, and washing; water and
      oxygen supplies; solar panels and batteries

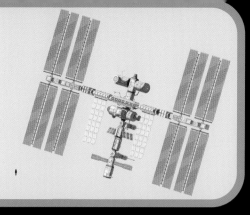

The 34-m-
(112-ft) long solar
panels can turn
to face the Sun.

Working Hard

Astronauts from 19 countries
have worked onboard the ISS.
They observe Earth and
space. They also work in four
science laboratories, run by
Europe, Japan, Russia, and
the United States.

Astronaut Sunita Williams holds a
home containing Nefertiti the spider
during an experiment to see how
spiders behave in space. Nefertiti
returned safely to Earth.

Spacecraft can
dock here to
unload astronauts
and supplies.

83

SPACE TELESCOPES

Space telescopes orbit the Earth or the Sun. From this location, their view is not spoilt by Earth's atmosphere or pollution. Space telescopes capture images of the whole sky or focus only on one area or object, such as the Sun.

The James Webb telescope orbits the Sun in Earth's shadow so it stays cool.

Seeing More

Our eyes can see only ordinary light, named visible light. This light is just one type of energy given off by stars, galaxies, and black holes. Space telescopes can also detect other types of energy, such as infrared, gamma rays, X-rays, and radio waves.

This image, taken by the Spitzer Space Telescope, shows the infrared energy given off by the death of a Sun-like star. Infrared energy can be felt by humans as heat.

It collects infrared energy from objects far across the Universe.

84

Observing the Sun

The Solar Dynamics Observatory orbits the Sun halfway between Earth and the star, where its view is never blocked. It watches the Sun's sudden bursts of energy, which can be seen as loops and flares from its surface.

This picture of the Sun was created from images taken by the Solar Dynamics Observatory. Each "slice" shows a different type of energy, which the telescope has converted into a form our eyes can see.

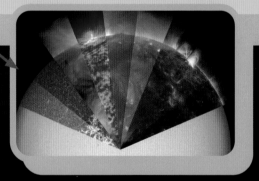

JAMES WEBB TELESCOPE
SIZE: 20 m (66 ft) long and 14 m (46 ft) wide
IN ACTION: From 2021
EQUIPMENT: Cameras that detect infrared and a 6.5-m (21-ft) main mirror for collecting light

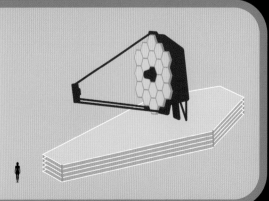

SPACE PROBES

Space probes are spacecraft that have no crew. They are robotic, which means they contain a computer that directs their activities. Some probes fly past other planets, moons, comets, and asteroids, while others orbit or land on them.

The *New Horizons* probe flew past the dwarf planet Pluto in 2015.

This radio antenna sends and receives information with Earth.

NEW HORIZONS

SIZE: 2.7 m (8.9 ft) long and 2.2 m (7.2 ft) wide

IN ACTION: From 2006

EQUIPMENT: three cameras, a dust sensor, and instruments to examine Pluto's atmosphere

Longest Journey

The probe *Voyager* 1 is the most distant human-made object, more than 23 billion km (14 billion miles) from Earth. After flying past Jupiter and Saturn, it left the Solar System in 2012. It still sends information back to Earth in the form of radio waves.

Voyager 1 set off in 1977. Its journey will continue for ever as there is nothing in space to stop its motion—unless it crashes into something.

A Closer Look

Orbiters are probes that orbit another planet or other space object. As they orbit, they take photos and collect information or even samples of dust. Orbiters have circled the Moon; the planets Mercury, Venus, Mars, Jupiter, and Saturn; four asteroids; and one comet.

From 2014 to 2016, *Rosetta* orbited the comet 67P/Churyumov-Gerasimenko, which measures only 4.3 by 4.1 km (2.7 by 2.5 miles).

LANDERS

There are two types of space probes: landers and impactors. Landers are probes that make a soft landing on another space object. In contrast, an impactor deliberately crashes into an object. The first successful lander was the Soviet *Luna 9*, which touched down on the Moon in 1966.

Bring it Home

Most landers stay at their destination, but some have collected samples of dust or rock then brought them home. Landers have returned samples from asteroids and the Moon. There are plans to return samples from Mars soon.

This illustration imagines the moment when the Japanese lander *Hayabusa* drilled into the asteroid Itokawa to collect dust.

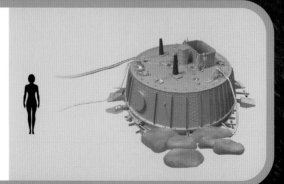

HUYGENS
SIZE: 2.7 m (8.9 ft) across
IN ACTION: 1997–2005
EQUIPMENT: Cameras and sensors to study wind, chemicals, and Titan's surface

Softly, Softly

Landers need to slow their fall to the surface and protect their instruments from the crash. As *Luna 9* fell toward the Moon, it fired small rockets to slow it down. When the bottom of the lander crashed into the surface, a ball-like landing capsule—containing its instruments—was popped out and rolled safely away.

This illustration shows *Luna 9* moments before landing on the Moon.

The *Huygens* probe landed on Saturn's moon Titan in 2005.

Information sent by *Huygens* told us that rain on Titan is methane—not water!

ROVERS

Rovers are robots with wheels. They can carry out tasks on their own, such as drilling into rocks and taking photos. We have sent rovers to explore the Moon, the planet Mars, and the asteroid Ryugu.

Studying Mars

In 1997, *Sojourner* was the first rover to land successfully on Mars. Rovers send information and photos as radio waves. The messages take up to 24 minutes to travel from Mars to Earth.

In 2021, a skycrane lowered the *Perseverance* rover onto Mars's Jezero Crater.

Perseverance's SuperCam identifies rock types from 7 m (20 ft) away.

Exploring the Moon

Rovers have been exploring the Moon since 1970. Moon rovers get their energy by turning sunlight into electricity using solar panels. At night, when it is dark, they power down—or take a sleep!

China's *Chang'e-3* lander photographed the *Yutu* rover as it rolled off on its mission, in 2013.

PERSEVERANCE
SIZE: 3 m (10 ft) long and 2.7 m (8.8 ft) wide
IN ACTION: From 2021
EQUIPMENT: 7 cameras, sensors, drills, and lasers

It uses a drill to see if there are signs of tiny life forms.

91

FUTURE MISSIONS

One day, humans could travel outside the Solar System. But using the rockets we have now, it would take us a thousand years to reach the nearest star! We would need food, water, and oxygen to breathe during the journey. For now, we will stay closer to home ...

The Launch Abort System pulls the capsule away from its rocket in an emergency.

The new Orion space capsule could carry humans to Mars.

Back to the Moon

Only 12 humans, all of them men, have walked on the Moon—and no one has set foot there since 1972. There are plans for humans, including at least one woman, to return to the Moon within the next 10 years.

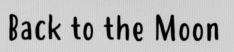

The United States plans to build a base on the Moon, where astronauts can live for months at a time.

ORION
SIZE: 6 m (19.7 ft) long and 5 m (16 ft) wide
IN ACTION: From 2022
EQUIPMENT: Seats, bunks, bathroom, engines, four computers, and 67 switches

Journey to the Red Planet

China, Europe, Russia, and the United States hope to send humans to Mars within the next 20 to 50 years. As Earth and Mars travel around the Sun, the shortest distance between them is 55 million km (34 million miles). The journey would take at least 7 months.

If astronauts built a base on Mars, they would need to take machines and materials to make water, oxygen, and food.

GLOSSARY

asteroid
A small rocky or metal object that orbits the Sun.

astronaut
A person who is trained to travel in a spacecraft.

astronomer
A scientist who studies the stars, planets, and other objects in space.

atmosphere
The gases that surround a planet or moon, held there by its gravity.

atom
The smallest part of any substance able to exist on its own.

average
A middle number or measurement, calculated by dividing the total of all the possible measurements by the number of measurements.

axis
An imaginary straight line through a planet or moon, around which the object turns.

black hole
An area of space with such strong gravity that no object—or light—can escape its pull.

comet
A small icy object with an elliptical (stretched-out) orbit that takes it both close to and far from the Sun.

conjunction
When two or more planets or other objects appear to be close together in the sky.

constellation
A group of stars that seem to make a pattern in the night sky, when viewed from Earth.

core
The innermost part of a planet, star, or moon.

counterclockwise
The opposite direction from the way the hands of a clock turn; also known as anticlockwise.

crater
A circular dip in the surface of a planet or moon, made by a space rock.

crust
The outer layer of a planet or moon.

day
The time taken for a planet to turn around its axis, so the Sun appears to return to the same position in the sky. Daytime is the portion of a day when a part of the planet is facing the Sun.

dense
Tightly packed.

dwarf planet
A rounded object that orbits a star but is not large enough for its gravity to clear other objects out of its orbit.

eclipse
When a star, planet, or moon is hidden by having another large object move between it and the watcher, or when it moves into the shadow of another object.

equator
An invisible line around the middle of a planet, dividing it into northern and southern halves.

exoplanet
A planet outside our Solar System.

galaxy
Thousands, millions, or billions of stars, as well as gas and dust, that are held together by gravity.

gas
A substance, such as air, that can move around freely and has no fixed shape.

gravity
A force that pulls all objects toward each other. The more massive the object, the stronger the pull of its gravity.

helium
The second most common type of atom in the Universe. Helium is a gas at a normal room temperature.

hemisphere
Half of a ball-shaped object, such as a planet or moon.

hydrogen
The most common type of atom in the Universe. Hydrogen is a gas at a normal room temperature.

infrared
A type of energy that is invisible to human eyes but can be felt as warmth.

lava
Melted rock after it has spilled out of a volcano.

light year
The distance that light travels in a year: 9.46 trillion km (5.88 trillion miles).

liquid
A substance that flows and can be poured.

magnetism
A force that pulls or pushes magnets toward or away from each other.

mantle
The layer inside a planet or moon that lies between the crust and the core.

mass
A measure of the amount of material in an object; also known as weight.

metallic
Behaving like a metal by letting electricity flow through it.

meteor
A portion of a comet, asteroid, or other space object that is glowing as it travels through Earth's atmosphere; also known as a shooting star.

meteorite
A portion of a comet, asteroid, or other space object that lands on Earth's surface.

moon
A large, rocky or icy object that orbits a planet; Earth has one moon.

orbit
The curved path of an object around a star, planet, or moon.

oxygen
The third most common type of atom in the Universe. Oxygen is a gas at a normal room temperature and is needed for life.

particle
A tiny portion of a substance.

plane
An imaginary flat surface.

planet
A large, rounded object that orbits the Sun or another star. Its gravity is strong enough to clear other objects out of its orbit.

pole
A point at the most northerly or most southerly end of a planet, moon, or star.

radio wave
A type of energy that can travel through space and be used for sending information. At one end, a radio transmitter "codes" the information into a radio wave by changing the wave's shape; at the other end, a receiver "decodes" the wave.

robot
A machine containing a computer that is programmed to carry out some of its activities independently.

rocket
A vehicle with a powerful engine that burns fuel to make a blast of hot gas, which sends the rocket in the opposite direction.

rotation
Turning around an axis.

rover
A robot that can travel across the surface of a planet, moon, or other space object.

satellite
A human-made object that is placed in orbit around a planet or moon. Any object that orbits a larger object may also be known as a satellite.

solar panel
A device that turns sunlight into electricity.

Solar System
The eight planets and the smaller rocky or icy objects that travel around the Sun.

space capsule
A wingless spacecraft, often used to carry a human crew.

spacecraft
A vehicle used for journeying in space.

space probe
A spacecraft that has no human crew.

space station
A large satellite that can be lived and worked in for long periods of time.

star
A huge ball of super-hot gas.

Sun
The star at the middle of our Solar System, around which Earth and the other planets orbit.

telescope
An instrument designed to make distant objects appear nearer, using mirrors and lenses to collect and focus light.

transit
When a planet or moon seems to move across the face of a larger object, covering a small portion of it.

Universe
All of space and its contents, including planets, stars, galaxies, and all other objects and energy.

visible Universe
The part of the Universe that we can see from Earth.

volcano
A hole in a planet or moon's surface through which melted rock named lava can spill out.

year
The time taken for a planet to complete one orbit around the Sun.

INDEX